T0198865

Reclaiming My Position is an inspiration to anyone that is facing challenges in life or unexpected trials. It is a story about knowing who you are intended to be and not allowing anything to claim your rightful place in the Kingdom of God. Paulina shares her personal life story thus far and in spite of the fiery darts, setbacks, rejections, and hurt she has reclaimed her position as a child of the Most High God. She lives unashamed of her past, because she knows the hands her today, tomorrow are in and that alone is enough to keep going forward and higher. My sister is unapologetic about her choices and mistakes, because out of the mess a living testimony, mighty praise, ministries, songs, and an inspiring story of life was birth.

Dena Taylor

Reclaiming My Position - A Heroic Message to Young Women is a short story written by Mrs. Paulina B .Cole Hardy. This short store depicts the life of the writer, her realization that growth can be very painful, traumatic, and uncomfortable, yet very necessary and essential to our wellbeing as God's creations.

Victor Cole

It is not often that one encounters an individual and you realize that there is something special about that person. This was the case when I met Paulina Abesordu Cole-Hardy. It did not take me long to realize that she was a lady of integrity and essence. Over the years, she has demonstrated that she is someone of honesty, pride, and dignity.

Having such character and personality is her strength. I am sure you will enjoy reading Mrs. Cole-Hardy's biography. You will definitely want to know how this woman of substance came into being.

I am grateful for her friendship and am very pleased to know her.

Vera B. Tolbert, MS, PhD

Reclaiming My Position is an unfolding, passionate conviction of a true child of God. Rev. Paulina Cole-Hardy unfolds her life story and experiences in a forceful fraction as directed by the Holy Spirit.

The readers will be on a journey with the author through the pages of this book, most of all experiencing the God given guidance and protection from the village of Africa to the cities of America. And it has all been possible by the grace of our mighty God!

Read this book and see what God can do with anyone who is willing to totally surrender to the will of God. May you continue to reclaim your position by following His plan for your life.

"Humble yourselves in the sight of the Lord, and He will lift you up."James 4:10

~ Bishop Nathan Kortu, Jr. ~

As she illustrates her life story in her book and preachings from her vast experiences with God, Rev. Paulina Cole-Hardy is committed to fearlessly and lovingly proclaim the word of God through the message in her book. For this reason, people are easily attracted to her because of her life experiences.

Pastor Zarwolo M. Gatei.

RECLAIMING MY POSITION

A Heroic Message to Young Women

Paulina Cole-Hardy

authorHOUSE®

AuthorHouse™
1663 Liberty Drive
Bloomington, IN 47403
www.authorhouse.com
Phone: 1 (800) 839-8640

Published by AuthorHouse 05/17/2018

ISBN: 978-1-5462-4138-6 (sc)
ISBN: 978-1-5462-4137-9 (e)

Library of Congress Control Number: 2018905772

Print information available on the last page.

Dedicated To:
My parents: Mr. Christopher T.S. Cole
and Mrs. Princess Beatrice Cole for being
wonderful parents out of this world.
Mr. Samuel H. Hardy, my Hubby for
your love and support without border
My children & grandchildren,
you are my inspiration
And the men and women of God that
have had influence on my life.

Introduction

Sometimes in life, the enemy will take you out of your God-given position and try to replace you. As a child of the Almighty God, you must pray for the spirit of discernment and the wisdom to know what your God-given position in his kingdom is. You must know why you are here on earth in the first place. The enemy tried to reposition me as a mother, a wife, a daughter, and a born-again believer. I had to reclaim what was legally mine as a child of God. There were several distractions along the way, but his grace was sufficient, and his strength was made perfect during it all.

"What does life have to do with it?" I write to clear the doubts and uncover the truth about my life. I write to make peace with myself and the things beyond my control that have transpired, and I have incurred over the years. I write to eliminate the deep pain of sadness and rejection I feel at times.

I write to unleash the saving grace and meaningful blessings that are bestowed on me and to reveal the beauty and greatness of our Lord's doing. Through life's journey, I have come to the realization that growth can be very painful, traumatic, and uncomfortable, yet very necessary and essential to our well-being as God creations.

I have no regrets nor make any apologies for the things I have done, encountered in life, or the decisions I have made in the past. Each moment, each encounter, each decision has only made me stronger and assured me that now *I can do all things, Through Christ who strengthens me, (Philippians 4:13 NKJV).*

My Scars

We all have our individual scars, but in the role of a leader, it is not an easy task to be transparent. It is not easy to talk about the things that you have walked through, currently walking through and will walk through. As a leader most of the time, we want to talk about how the congregation can be blessed, how they can be free from the grips of the enemy, how they can receive redemption, and how they can be blessed with the favor of God. It is an infrequent leader that will reveal his or herself to the world. Regardless of what your status or position is, no man or woman is immune to the strike of the enemy. The enemy is no respecter of persons, he will strike at any time, anywhere, anyhow. We all have our scars in different places and with different experiences, and all our scars tell our individual stories as I am telling mine.

As you read *RECLAIMING MY POSITION,* you will realize that even I as a preacher, ministering the gospel of good news has had and is still experiencing the attack from the enemy on a constant basis. The journey has not been smooth sailing, but with God from whom my strength is made perfect, even when I am weak, He continues to guide and protect me through it all. God has afforded me the ability to conquer the attacks of the devil and reclaim my position in his kingdom.

As you indulge in the pages of my life, I pray that you see your own struggles through mine and avoid being judgmental and that you do not allow pride to set in your heart. I hope you may realize that my faith taking a blow does not mean I am faithless. I am no different from those that get hit with unfortunate situations, sickness, disappointment, and more in life, yet when my faith is tested, I stay strong and keep standing. As the bible rightly said, *"Take unto you the whole armor of God, that ye may be able to withstand in the evil day and having done all, to STAND".* Ephesians 6:13

You have made the golden choice by purchasing this book, as the title, states RECLAIMING MY POSITION; I pray you will receive some of the needed tools to assist you in reclaiming your position as a child of God by taking this journey with me.

HOW IT ALL
STARTED

Brief Family Background

I was born unto the beautiful union of two people who fell in love very early in their lives. Mr. Christopher Tarwo Shafume Cole and Mrs. Princess Beatrice Norman Kpandebah Cole, natives of Liberia, West Africa. I was born in one of the many beautiful cities of Liberia and at one of the best hospitals at the time in Yekepa,-Nimba Co. Liberia West Africa, a county endowed with numerous natural riches and wonders such as forestry, iron ore, diamonds, gold, beautiful rivers and streams, to name a few. Interestingly, where I was born carried the acronym of a mining company LAMCO, which stands for Liberia American Mining Company.

I came from a musical family that has a history of musicians. My late grandmother was a traditional musician who played an instrument called "SASA". My deceased father was a musical genius; he owned a band which he directed for several years and he could play numerous instruments. I fondly remembered him playing the guitar and singing on a regular basis, while my siblings and I sang along. We were also members of the Mount Nimba Baptist Church choir located in Area A, Yekepa, Nimba County.

My family was very strong on spiritual and educational values. We had weekly devotions and went to church every Sunday. We participated in the girl's axillaries, choir, team time quizzes, Sunday school, prayer meetings, and mid-week services, Christmas plays, and other related church activities. We were taught to work hard for the things we desire in life, and not to envy others for what they have achieved. During the weekdays we had family devotion every morning, at which time we will recite the Lord's Prayer and the 23rd psalms. Not only did my family instill spiritual values during our devotion time, but my parents also would reinforce the importance and value of having an education. My dad would tell us "I have no wealth stored out for you. All I ask of you all is to work hard, get as much education as you can to fulfill your dreams, let the sky be your limit."

When it came to school and furthering our education, we had no option, but to keep going for the best and reaching for the skies. My family values have helped shaped my life, even today I am the woman I am because of those values instilled in me from childhood.

My beautiful mother Princess that we affectionately called Ma Cece; she alluded to me that during her conception with me was a time of transition. She and my dad had just moved to a new city called Yekepa, Nimba Co. in pursuit of greener pastures for their growing family. My father later got employment with the Lamco Mining Co. where he worked and served for 25 years before retiring.

My mother explained to me that giving birth to me was normal and that my development from infancy, to preschool, and early adolescent years was normal. I grew as a normal child with both parents at home caring for my siblings and me. My parents both worked 8-hour shifts; they were usually gone from 8:00 AM to 4:00 PM daily and off on the weekends. My mother worked as an executive secretary to the President of the Liberia Swedish Vocational Training Center (LSVTC) in LAMCO, while my father worked as the director of the recreational facility.

My father also owned and served as one of the professors at the Cole's Institute of Short Hand and basic secretarial science courses, the school taught Gregg and Pitman shorthand to executive secretary's, office managers, and assistants, he also directed a ten members band for many years.

Preschool Years

My preschool years was fun-filled, I attended a private Catholic school where I experienced the unfolding of my imagination and discovered my enthusiasm to be a part of the different school activities. It was overwhelmingly clear to my parents and teachers that I did not need a dull moment in my day and I needed to be involved.

I danced Ballet, was a part of the kids cheerleading team, and the kid's egg race team. I also became a part of the kid's Spelling Bee. There are a few childhood memories that have stayed with me over the years. One incident that resonates with me till present happened around Christmas time one year.

I was a part of the bally dance team that was to perform at that Christmas program. We wore beautiful peach colored tops, white skirts with bloomers, white tennis shoes, and white socks.

While the music played, and we did our dance moves, I wanted to visit the restroom. I called out to the teacher, but she did not hear me on two occasions due to the loud sound of the music.

Suddenly, I then felt a warm liquid down my leg and I right away knew what it was, but that did not stop me from doing my moves, I completed the dance moves and complained after.

I also remembered going to school and being called to the front of the class by the teacher we called Ms. Gertrude who is still alive at the time of writing this book, lives in the New Jersey area. She would instruct me to write from A to Z on the chalkboard, help with the class work, and read to the class. Humbly, I was a smart kid and could catch on to class work and activities very quickly than others. I was advanced one class at the age of eight and I still received a promotion at the end of the school calendar year.

I can vividly recall another incident; my parents had a guest over at the house. While they were conversing, I realized the guy had one ear; his other ear had been cut off and that made me very curious. So, I thought to ask what went wrong with the other ear.

I proceeded to ask the question when my dad blinked at me and said no. I insisted and finally asked, that was one embarrassing moment for the guy and my parents. He finally told me the story that led to him having one ear. But kids will be kids, right? That truly was a moment for all that were involved.

At the end of the school year, I was promoted to the first grade and stayed in that school for two more years and was promoted to the 4th grade and it was time to change school. The company my father worked for Liberia American Mining Company (LAMCO) a courtesy to their employees, they built homes of various communities for their employees and name them after the twenty-six alphabets from area A to Z. My parents lived in area A, but I went school in area C.

I started 4th grade at Area C- School in the afternoon from 12:00 PM till 5:00 pm, the school had two sessions morning and afternoon, I stayed in area C- school till part of my ninth-grade year and part of ninth grade I was completed at the adult night school located in area B.

I still remember the names of a few of my first through ninth grade teacher, Ms. Lucy, Mr. Togba, Mrs. Rogers, Mr. Clarke, and Mr. Jap Wright. Mr. Wright was hilarious, he would tell us different life stories that were humorous but give the class reasons to think. Interestingly, he will at times substitute names of characters in stories by the names of his students which was so captivating. At the end of the school day, he would say "All things been equal, in the absence of no more question, you are dismissed." He had a slogan that said, "There are many ways to kill a cat."

Elementary school was awesome, we ate Kala- a locally made rounded shape bread but very little in size, drank skim milk, and at times had cornmeal on Fridays. we looked forward to every Friday because of the meal that was prepared for us.

Our school day would get started with the students lining up in the courtyard to say their morning prayers and to pledge their allegiance to the country's flag. This time was also used to carry out disciplinary actions for students who disobeyed the school codes of conduct. After this morning routine, we will all leave for our assigned classrooms.

There were many school challenges I encountered. I recalled being bullied many times, I was told how short I was, how tomboyish I looked, and how there was nothing Girley about me. I was challenged to tell whoever I wished to complain to, but I would pay for telling after, out of fear I always ran to the bus.

One day after school, I was chased down a stream that was located at the back of the school fence and was jumped into a fight, but this time I gathered some courage and decided to fight back. My cup was filled with being bullied; I was tired of always running and losing the fight. I fought and fought, but again I lost the fight, I was ashamed and began to give excuses to stay away from school, I was afraid to tell anyone what was happening, not even my parents for fear of getting beaten badly the next time I got jumped into a fight. My only choice then was to keep things to myself and find a way to defeat this giant, but it wasn't just the giant to face to bullying but having the self-confidence to speak out on other ills. The greatest challenge was if I couldn't stand up to speak against a thing that I was confronted with, how gallant could I have been to speak against ills affecting others.

As time went by, the company, assigned buses to the school to take students home. As a result, I couldn't easily see my bullies after school. The bus driver assigned to my bus was a lover of kids and an interesting character. One of his recognizable identities was one gold tooth in the front of his mouth. Interestingly, he was a driver that would hold his breaks several times during our drive to and from school. His action ignited songs in us. We would sing songs of his name. One of the songs sung for him as I can remember went like this "Open teeth wa wa co wa, wa co wa; colored boy wa wa co wa, wa co wa."

Periodically, I would see them in the hallway or at times on the school activities field. Every time we saw each other, something was said that would get under my skin, but I would not respond or react to any of the snares.

This is what bullying does, it makes the one being bullied feels inferior and intimidate to face his or her scoffer. However, I still had to stand up and face this issue – to put an end to it. It was a beautiful Thursday morning the ray of the sun had brightened my day and I was optimistic about all I had to do that day but there was a sudden anger that rose up in me saying "this must end." There are some things about our lives that will not change if we don't get angry about it. This was one! I said to myself "either I allow the bullies to keep bulling me or the bullying must come to an end today, as I was prepared to fight for my freedom."

Remember, there are some issues you can be diplomatic about and others you must be radical about and bullying was one to be radical about especially living in a nation where the issue of bullying was not addressed to the teeth or there wasn't any media discussion, it was a norm to live with. My approach to end being bullied was sample though it was not the best choice and I wouldn't recommend anyone using this approach; it worked for me. I prepared some crushed pepper mixed with water to create a pepper spray-like that I would use in my fight day. I went to school with this pepper spray-like tool which I kept on me all day, and everywhere I went on campus because I was prepared to stop my bully. Luckily for me came my scoffer with the hateful words as usual, when I tried to respond she jumped me again into a fight because she would always win, but it was different on this day. I held behind me the pepper spray and as the fight started, I used my paper spray and at that point, I had the upper hand. Few of kids that hung around begin to cheer me up. While the fight was on, the news spread like wildfire. The entire student body had come to see the fight but no one came to separate the fight. I did what was always done to me; the authorities of the school finally came. Henceforth, from that day forward my bullies never crossed my path and I received my freedom.

ADOLESCENCE

Remarkable Memories

Growing up was fun at times but not so much fun. I grew up in a home with my six siblings, of which I am the fifth child of seven children. Although we had a large family, my parents had a way of making each of us feel special. I remembered many Saturdays my dad would take my younger sister and me for a spin on his Vesper Bike to the ice cream shop to get a treat of ice cream. My dad would make a fist and ask us to undo it, then he would also stretch out his muscular arms and ask us to swing back and forth on his arms. Oh, what beautiful memories. He was a great storyteller and an awesome comedian. Most of the time, he would cheer up the family with laughter. These were special moments of my life.

Peer Pressure

Peer pressure has been a very strong force that many teenagers faced and I am not an exception. Between ages, thirteen and fourteen of my life, many of my friends were discussing sex. Some already knew what it was all about although they have not experienced it. Absolutely, I knew nothing about sex, neither have I heard anything of it so I was considered "green", an urban term used by young Liberians to imply ignorance or the lack of understanding.

Between grades seventh and ninth, my friends and classmates will be discussing sex topics. Whenever they are in gathering discussing and see me approaching, they would change their discussion to something else. All their fronting did last long enough because they wanted to know if I knew about sex or have had any experience. When they realized I had no idea and no input, then bullying started in another form. They would call me Holy Mary,

Jesus daughter, Christian girl, pastor, and so forth. They sometimes drove me from their companies or ask that I do not participate in their conversations because I had no input. It got to a point I began to feel pressure, the pressure of wanting to be on the same pace with them, the pressure of wanting to have an input by having my share of experience, the pressure of not feeling a part of their clique and the pressure of acceptance by my peer.

I was experiencing peer pressure from an unfamiliar perspective, it wasn't the pressure of clubbing, smoking, drinking alcohol, or doing other indecent stuff. In fact, in the 60s in which I was born very little or nothing was known about drugs amongst my peers, the community, or society. There was not much information on drug and addiction in my community. We really did not hear of any type of drugs being used, abused, or what effect it had on the abusers.

The major challenge during my mid-adolescence years was the pressure of sexual experience. I became victimized after years of protecting my innocent mind and virginity and living up to the teaching of the church on abstinence. I was that girl that believed abstinence was the way to go, that there be no sex before marriage, as the scripture speaks, *"Acts 15:20, abstain from fornication."*

The morals on how a promising young lady should conduct herself, dress modestly, and live up to the spiritual values instilled in her were clear, but the pressure of being different was immense. I was that girl who kept her innocence of the mind and had the audacity to keep her virginity. I was considered the naive one, the one who was not sophisticated enough to be seen and liked by those that were sexually active. The odds were against me and I felt all alone. I was isolated from sexual conversations; my peers try to ridicule me if I tried speaking on said topic because my position on sexual immorality was different from theirs.

As far as my contemporaries were concerned, I knew nothing about sex, so why I speak of anything in that category. They talked about me, scorned at me, and sometimes ask me "who do you think you are?" I was bullied that resulted in fights at times. I was bullied because of not wanting to have sex before getting married, "WHAT A CRIME RIGHT" to commit.

As the pressure mounted, I thought about different options that could ease the tension or stop it completely. My thoughts ran from wanting to change school, or just give in to be left alone.

In my earliest teen, I met a young man who was about a year older than me. He was the son of one of my dad's business associates who lived in the same area we lived after my dad's retirement. He told me he loved me and that he wanted me to be his ideal girlfriend, that was the name at the time, IDEAL GIRLFRIEND. Therefore, we started talking and dating; I would go and see him every now and then on my way to catch the bus for school. He began whispering in my innocent ears and will tell me how pretty I was, how much he loved and cared for me, and that he will make me his wife. Due to the ever-increasing peer pressure at school from friends and classmates coupled with the heartfelt words of this young man that was overwhelming, I started to have second thoughts.

In fact, everyone else around me between the ages of 15-18, at the time has already had experienced sex except for few others including myself. Friends and classmates were talking about sex in my presence on purpose that made me very uncomfortable. They would write sexually explicit notation in my notebooks and textbooks, leave notes on my desk, and had fun humiliating me and others who were still holding on to their spiritual values and virginity. This became unbearable that I started to reconsider my decision.

At the age of seventeen, I became a victim of peer pressure. I had intercourse with the handsome young man who told me all the nicest things at the time in the world. I did not know where to start; it was an awkward moment when he told me he was experiencing sex for the second time, but I had no idea of what I was doing. I finally became prey to the experience of sex that haunted me through my peers for so long, because from that first experience I got pregnant and he fathered my first child.

For the first time, I knew not what to feel, to do or expect. I had no idea what I was doing or getting myself involved with. After that experience I did not partake anymore in sex; I started to ask myself what I was supposed to do or say. However, months went by and the mixed feelings of not being much of myself as well as having an outburst attitude, mad about everything, feeling sleepy all the time, and always craving different food, I was not sure what was happening to me.

My teacher and the school nurse noticed a change in my behavior and participation in class and they decided to notify my mother. Beforehand, she had her own suspicion of the rapid growth in my abdominal area, my choice of food, and my constant complaining of tiredness, but she never said a word.

My situation was of a serious concern to my teacher and the school nurse that it resulted in a doctor's visit which was set up by my mother with the consent of the school nurse. Two days later, I was in for a complete checkup. It was when I became fully aware that I was four months pregnant. I was about to become a teen mother.

Oh my God (OMG) this was a shocker and was considered a crime at the time. I could not imagine how I was going to live with this. This was the last news I wanted to hear. I wonder over and over in my innocent mind – asking myself how I got here, what have I done to my parents, my siblings, and myself. I was lost, afraid, ashamed, and felt so helpless and hopeless. I felt I had disappointed my entire family, especially my parents who were known for their high moral standards in the community. WHAT HAVE I DONE, gosh!!!!!!!

When the news of my pregnancy finally got to the school and the community, my feeling of being hopeless increased. Other parents told their virgin daughters to stay away from me to avoid them from going down the same path as I did. That even broke me more. Many had said I was not a good example. I was devastated and tormented by what I was hearing and what was happening around me. It was a time in our society, Liberia, West Africa when teenage pregnancy and abortion was on the rise amongst teenage girls; their decision at times resulted in the death of both the mothers and their unborn babies.

In my time, young women were using different abortion methods to avoid the embarrassment. In those days, technology and medicine were in their preliminary stages as researchers worked to find different and new cures for existing disease, the world was becoming innovative in medicine but not sophisticated enough to take on the huge challenges of modern health.

My experience of teen pregnancy was a very difficult time in my life, and very disappointing for my parents, especially my dad who was well respected and known for his spiritual values in our community, the organization he affiliated with, and the church. I was shamefaced to a point that I had thoughts of running away to avoid the ridicule and isolation I was getting from my peers. It was painful to be avoided by the only group of people you have known all your life. Thus, I was lonely, scared, ashamed, and uncomfortable. But I always wondered what my baby would look like will she look like me or, what my baby would feel like in my arms for the first time, what will I want to say to my baby, those were some questions I thought about.

I vividly remembered on one occasion I felt at the lowest point of my life because I was filled with so much guilt and remorse within myself that I needed someone to talk to. My oldest brother was down visiting for the weekend, who was informed of my pregnancy, came to have a talk with me as a big brother. I then decided to open to him about how I felt at that moment. He said these words to me "You are not the first teenager to get pregnant and you will not be the last, you have your whole life ahead of you to make it beautiful again what has happened is done, you cannot change the situation, so make the best of it and take care of yourself."

He was very positive and gave me the assurance that there is life after teenage pregnancy, there is always room for growth and maturity, and there is always a light at the end of a tunnel. I was reassured. From that moment, I knew that life was not over for me, that I can be the beautiful woman that God had created me to be. God will always, always send a guiding angel to bring you words of comfort during the time you need him the most. Mistakes can be made in our lives, but we cannot allow those mistakes to determine our future, we can always turn those testing times through the word of God into our testimonies and our testimonies can encourage others who find themselves going through the same situation we were once faced with.

Effect and Support

The effect of being ashamed of my decision had caused me to become very withdrawn and the feeling of depression. From the decision and advice of the school, I had to withdraw from daytime high school and continued at the adult night school.

This environment was all new and very embarrassing for my family and me. It was not a place of comfort for me at all. By accepting the fact that I am in school with individuals that were older was never a welcoming situation. Though it reduced the tension of mockery from my peers, yet it brought a new kind of stress and discomfort. The tension gradually faded away as it is often said: "time heals." I began to settle in and make the most of it, I try to stay focus and continued my schooling

After months of uncertainty, anxiety, and being anxious about what God was creating in my belly, the long-awaited night finally arrived on January 31st, 1980 at 12:30 AM. I gave birth to a beautiful baby girl named Laila Princess Hamdan, now Mrs. Smith.

The next morning my dad, Mr. Christopher T. S. Cole came to visit me at the hospital. He held the baby for hours, singing to her as he rocked her back and forth in the easy chair. It was a relief for me having him over. I assumed I had been somehow forgiven and could now put the situation behind me. I was finally able to catch a nap after the night of hours of labor pain and staying awake to care for my newborn. After days at the hospital, my parents and siblings were all excited and welcomed the baby and me home. The frustration I carried was not geared towards having my daughter because I loved her from the moment I laid eyes on her. She was a beautiful bundle of joy God had entrusted me with, and I would not have traded that moment for anything in this world. She was my baby who made me see life from a different perspective. Because of her, I could now be celebrated as a mother; despite all the challenges during my pregnancy. I am proud to be her mother, today we continued to improve our relationship that was abruptly interrupted by the enemy years ago.

My spiritual values instilled in me by my parents helped me during my recovery process. I remembered attending church during a prayer meeting; at that meeting, I was reminded that God was not mad at me, He is a God who forgives and that He only wanted me to repent, and that He was able to heal my hurting heart.

My strongest support came right before and after the baby was born from some family members, the church, and a few other people from the community; they were there for me whenever I needed them. I made up my mind to visit the church often. Though the challenges were there with the newborn present, I kept my course to continue my education; and completed the ninth grade. It is very necessary to have that support group in your space, because you will need them at one point or the other, having a support system in times of uncertainties is very important, a support system can be made of anyone who is willing to be there for you, to see you through those times of difficulties.

Life was back to normal again, and I remembered there was a traditional wedding going on in my neighborhood on a Saturday evening. People from the community including myself decided to go witness the ceremony. While the ceremony was going on, I did not have a pleasant view from where I was standing so I moved to the other side where there was an old oil container laying on the floor. I turned it upside down and climbed on the top for a better view.

Caught in the moment of the ceremony, I began to feel the wind under my skirt; I turned around and saw a young man about my age peeping under my skirt with a piece of wood he quietly used to lift my skirt. I got furious and hit him with my left leg, and I suddenly lost my balance and fell to the ground. Quickly, I got up and questioned the guy about what he did, he jumped me into a fight; I hit him, and he started bleeding from his nostril and someone came and separated us. It can be inferred that I won, but I knew it was not over because his parents knew mine. Later that evening, the boy's parents came to my home and told my mother what had taken place at the wedding. My parents perceived that my tomboyish behavior, not being afraid of anything and anyone would lead me to a bigger problem, so they made the decision to send me away for high school. Boarding school life experience began for me.

I was going away for four years to attend the Booker Washington Institute known as BWI for short, a vocational training high school that was about 8 hours away from home. BWI was a boarding school for both girls and boys; its dorms were separated and fenced. we could see the boys during our class time and on weekends only. We were restricted from going to the boy's dorms and likewise. I was only allowed to come home for visit on some weekends and holidays. The school was very strict about its rules. No joke!

I had to learn to make decisions on my own, manage my time, and be responsible for my wellbeing. My elder sisters were products of the school who graduated and left indelible marks. This was a wakeup call for me.

One remarkable policy the school had was to allow senior students take disciplinary actions on freshman, sophomore, and junior students. Senior students gave punishment/assignment for every decision I made that was not right. they told me stories about how my sisters made them clean, scrub, did laundry and did some of the very punishment/assignment they were making me do. I would cry while I did my punishment/assignment. This happened so often that I begin to grow thick skin until; it did not mean much to me any longer. I became rebellious and after a while, they got tired and would leave me for months, without being assigned to any chores, and would start all over again.

I made new friends during my time on campus and I also reconnected with some friends from elementary school that were on campus. This was life at the boarding school.

Adulthood

I was able to continue my education through high school; I graduated went on to college. After graduation, my friends and I grew very close over the years. I got stuck with one who is still my best friend till present, Lena father and my father worked for the same company, LAMCO. We lived not far from one another and were always together. We got in troubles together and received consequences for our actions together. Wherever she was seen, I was right next to her and vice versa.

While on BWI, we made three other friends: Amy, Rebecca, and Joyce. We formed a girl athletic group called "HOT APRIL" it stood for the initials of our first names; we are all still friends today.

We played on the school volleyball and kickball teams; we were also members of the school cheering squad. Our class '84' brought great excitement to the school team. During our years at

Booker Washington Institute, we kept the school championship going in all sports for the four years we were on campus.

Lena is that friend that I could share anything and everything with. We had no secrets. We all have a friend with no limits when it comes to sharing our thoughts and feelings. Lena was that friend! It is always to have the one person in your corner, the one you share everything, even your secrets with, it is relieving to have that someone you can confide in.

After graduating from high school, I went on to the University of Liberia (LU) as a part-time student. Lena and I moved to the city, Monrovia where we lived a few blocks away from each other. As adults, we made time to hang out, have lunch dates, and girls time together, till we were separated by the civil crisis in our country, Liberia.

First Marriage Experience

On my way home after one of my midterms, I reconnected with a guy who was crazy about me during my senior year on BWI. We thought we were in love, not knowing what love really meant; we were excited to be together and it was beautiful in the beginning. After months of courtship, we were engaged and I got pregnant with my second daughter whom I called my dark chocolate, Ms. Kathleen. We immediately set time to after meeting my parents. After the baby came, we prematurely got married, I said prematurely because we both did not know what to expect, we really did not know what we were doing or getting into. I was at the young age of 22. We had a beautiful wedding with family and friends in attendance. I was not sure what I was getting myself into, nor did I realize the responsibilities I was about to take on.

Our union brought us three lovely children: Kathleen, Joshua, and Paul. Here we are with four kids of ours and four from his previous relationship of which the youngest two came to live with us. It was overwhelming for a young woman still in her twenties, never been married, no experience, with six young kids to care for. What was I thinking? I began to question myself. I felt like the "old woman who lived in the shoe who had so many children and didn't know what to do (Nursery Rhyme, 1794) I was about to grow up real fast!

The relationship lasted for about 12 years. Between the first 5 to 7 years brought tons of experiences and challenges. I began to feel trapped with lingering insecurities. My ex-husband had issues that lead us into fights and then he would later beg for forgiveness. He would reassure me of how much he loved me and that what he did was out of anger not hate. Oh yes, I believed him.

Our culture did not allow room for women to have much say in their homes. If you were married then, your partner could question your faithfulness without any reason, could abuse you physically and mentally or could do whatever he wishes as a man without being questioned. Women's rights were the last thing on the agenda for our lawmakers at the time.

My marriage began to go south due to the stress, anger, anxiousness, and uncertainties; it made me feel very fragile. I was wasting away and wondered what my future would be if I stayed. While in an ocean of thoughts on what decision to make, we began to hear news of the war from various news media in the country.

The Civil Unrest

I turned on the news one evening in December of 1989 and I heard about the uprising that had started in my country. Rebels had infiltrated the country and were headed for the city where we lived. After months of intensive fighting, they made it into the city and took over a large area; we were now under their control.

The city was curfewed from 7 AM till 7 PM daily. If you were caught outside between those times as a civilian, you are dead. The rebels used that time to loot businesses and homes.

It was terrifying for me being caught in the middle of two crises: the nation deadly civil crisis and the domestic crisis of constant fear for my life and the lives of my children, therefore, resulted in my decision to do something different. I have longed to be a free woman again- wanting to experience a sense of peace and love for life without physical and mental torture but just learning what true love is all about. I craved to be treated like a queen that God took His precious time to create and not to be looked upon as nobody. I wanted to know what being loved, felt, held and touched - feeling a sense of security.

That relationship ended and the process of finding peace and a place of rest from the sounds of grenades launchers, guns of various kinds, and chanting was what I begin to pursue.

Before the civil crisis in my nation, my older siblings had left the country for the United States to further their education. They had been in the United States for several years. My mother had returned from visiting the USA and months later she returned home just to be caught up in the civil crisis.

We were badly affected, we had no food, no water, even the clothes on our backs were shredding. The shoes on our feet were destroyed from many miles of walking from place to place in search of food, shelter, and safety. The condition became so stressful. My kids began to get sick due to malnutrition, my son Josh at the time was about two years of age. I remembered he was so sick he could not eat; he was losing weight very fast, I did not know what to do, there were no doctors, hospital, no medical facility in operation. Everything in sight was destroyed, either by fire, water or looting. We were left with no other alternatives but to begin seeking refuge in different towns, villages, cities, and at times nearby countries if possible.

During our refuge search, we located a small town called Johnsonville, a town not very far from the City of Monrovia where we met an old man who lived in an abandoned building. He occupied the only room that had a window and door. We asked if we could stay there for some time and he allowed us to stay for as long as we could. The rest of the house had no window, no bed, no chair, no front door, no kitchen, no restroom, but an old bathroom that was located on the outside. The house was just an opened unfinished house. We were surrounded by trees, tall grasses, and bushes. We were vulnerable to the evil that was taking so many lives and devastating the country, the civil unrest.

It was that same evil that hunted our minds from the sounds of machine guns, grenade launchers, fifty caliber rifles, bazooka launchers, and other deadly weapons the warring factions used to destroy our beautiful and peaceful country.

We were in the open night and day without protection, our safety was at stake, the rebels came whenever they felt to do so, when they came they will take what looked good in their eyes. We were gasping for air every time we saw them, our kids will be clinging onto to our bodies, our teenage daughters will run into the bushes to hide because they could be taken away by the rebels at any time, they will be taken as hostages to be used as sex slaves, cooks, child soldiers, we have no say in those situations.

We were in that place for about two months and the condition worsens, the rebels visit became regular. They came with treats and it was fearful, frustrating and traumatic to stay around. At that point, I decided to join the rest of the Internally Displaced Population, IDP for short on the newly constructed sub-campus of the country's number one university, the University of Liberia, Fendell Campus.

For about three months into the crisis, I started having thoughts of relocation with my young children, we began to seek means of transportation to areas that were said to be safer than others but traveling with babies in a war situation is unthinkable. I feared the worst, unnecessary killings were everywhere, and the number of individuals displaced was ever increasing. We would be in total darkness at night and will hear cries of people being taken away from amongst us to be slaughtered. It was fearful, the killing was overwhelming: babies, elderly, women and men, there were no exceptions/considerations.

My family had lost everything we ever worked for – our home, car, businesses, etc. Life seemed meaningless at the time. I just wanted all the chaos to stop. I prayed every day that God would bring an end to the civil crisis. I just wanted the country to be at peace again, but that did not seem to be forthcoming, it was far for ending. The situation became overbearing that one could feel fear at the very thought of making a single move from the situation.

Trauma

The first sign of war happened on November 12th, 1985, when the late General Thomas Quiwonkpa planned coup-d'état failed, the situation was quickly put under control by the government. We were reassured of public safety and life seemed to be normal again but not for long. Although life seems to be normal, there was a cloud of tension over the country which birthed the nation civil crisis that started in December 1990. It was a civil crisis involving the government forces and the rebel forces, led by Charles G. Taylor, former President of Liberia who is currently facing sentence for 50 years in the Hauge by the World Crime Court. Things escalated with the formation of different rebel faction groups. The war affected so many families including mine.

We were victimized by the killings of friends, families, and looting, characterized by the disgruntled behavior of the rebel factions.

We experienced so many sleepless nights, going to bed without food and water for days. I watched my young children at the time their ages ranging from 1 ½, 5, 7, and 10, years of age, go to bed without food for 2 to 4 days at times. Surviving by just drinking water or milk and bread when we could afford or locate those items.

There were not any formal means of transportation available; therefore, walking for miles to get from one point to another in search of food, water or shelter was our only option. Those were dangerous times for a family that was so vulnerable, a family with very young children, no sense of direction, no money and no food. We just had to always be in survival mood.

The possibility of being caught between rebel factions in a shootout was evident and losing family members in the process and or contracting different kinds of deadly disease was of a high risk. We had to stay in camps in open fields, sleeping on floors of unfinished buildings, abandoned houses or shelters crowded with people for days, weeks, months at times, taking a shower was a privilege, we will walk for miles to get muddy well water and will have to let it set for an hour before using it to shower. At times, we went without a shower for days due to fear of getting hit by a strayed bullet, what a feeling.

My children suffered malnutrition that resulted in Kwashiorkor, they were bitten by mosquitoes, bed bugs, and they got lice in their hairs from sleeping in places that were not conducive for living. It was at that point I realized we were heading for trouble if I did not take a stand for my family, we would all die. Like Esther and Deborah in the Bible, I decided to do something to save my family; I made a prompt decision to leave the war-torn nation at the time and find refuge in neighboring countries.

At this junction, all I had in my mind was to get food, shelter and some health assistance for my children and me. We began the process of finding information on how we could be transported from where we were to where we were trying to relocate. It took us about two months to leave the Fendell campus, an extension of the University on foot to Kakata. We would stop in towns spend a night or day and continue our journey, it was devastating and very hard on our legs/feet, the kids would cry that we will have to carry them on our backs or arms, it was traumatic, writing about it brings back painful memories. But I am so grateful that we made it at last by the grace of God. We finally made it to Kakata and it was chaotic, rebels were everywhere in the streets, they had taken over businesses, schools, offices, hospitals and some individual homes.

A moment came when we were trying to get to a family member's home, not knowing what to expect; we were stopped by a female rebel. She requested to speak with my oldest daughter Laila. As Laila walked towards her, she pulled her closer and said this is my daughter now, you can leave with the other kids. I could not imagine leaving my daughter with a person who was so inhuman. At that point, I was ready to die; the disadvantage was just over the top for me. I prayed, "Lord I did not bring my kids this far to lose one, show yourself, Lord, once more. You have protected us thus far now you will see us through." *As* Psalm 140:1 says "Rescue me, O LORD, from evil men; Preserve me from violent men."

With boldness, I said I was not leaving without my daughter and we began to argue. I looked over my shoulder and saw a face that reminded me of someone I knew. It was that of an old friend and schoolmate, he screamed my name "PC!" as I was affectionately called by my peers during high school days. He came over to me and gave me a big hug and asked me what was going on. I explained the situation. He commanded the female rebel to return my daughter to me immediately and she did. I did not realize he was carrying the title of a General because he was fighting, but God rescued my daughter that day. It was traumatic, but God intervened.

We found the family member and spent two days in Kakata. God's promises are sure and true; He makes provisions where there is none, again He made a way, I knew he would come through and he did.

I came across another schoolmate called SLY; he recognized me immediately even though I looked very awful, I had lost so much weight, I was tiny from starvation, fear, and the unknown. He asked if my family and I were ok, and I said, "kind of." I told him what my intention was, which was to leave the country due to the unrest and ambivalences. He then shook my hands and left me with the first $100.00-dollar bill after several months of not seeing one. As the Apostle Paul rightly stated "and my God will supply every need according to his riches in glory by Christ Jesus" – Philippians 4:19.

Pain of Losing A Child

After spending a couple of days in the town Kakata, I then moved with my kids to another town called Boing Mines, a place named after a German-owned company. My children and I got to the town and were astonished. This place was about a four-hour drive from the city Monrovia where we had come from, a city destroyed so badly with gross darkness over its deep for months, where many had lost their lives. Coming to town and seeing almost everything, hospitals, supermarkets, and other businesses still intact and operating as normal was a complete shock to us. Especially, considering the Germans had left Bong Mines and the rebels were in control yet everything was left untouched, that was unbelievable. We lived peacefully in Bong Mines for a week, then I got a message that my mother and younger siblings were also in Bong Mines. We searched and located them on the other side of the town.

After reconnecting with my mother, she decided to journey to another county, Lofa County another part of the country that was a bit quiet from the crisis. People were in search of a peaceful place, a place free of the crisis and chaos. My mother took with her my younger siblings and had asked my permission to take my oldest daughter, Laila.

With the assistance of my foster brother – Soko, they were able to find a transportation that was willing to take them all at once. I considered that a smart move, because days after their departure, we were under siege again from the warring factions. Another rebel group had made it to Bong Mines and an intense fight started that had us barricaded for days. My frail body grew weary because of fear; I was weak, dehydrated, and felt like I was losing my mind.

One morning I visited the marketplace and while trying to get some food, I felt dizzy and passed out. Later, I found myself at home and asked what had happened, but the story explained to me made me think that it was due to me being anemic, only because I had always had the problem with weakness; I came to the realization that I was almost three months pregnant.

When you are going through a coarse time in your life filled with so much fear and anxiety, it affects different parts of your body. When I knew that I was pregnant, I wondered how this happened, why now, and asked myself what next because I barely had enough for me and the kids. How will I care for myself and the unborn? Again, I turned to the only one I knew could take care of me, God. According to Psalm 16:1-2, states "Protect me oh Lord for indeed do I put my trust. I said to the Lord, you are my Lord. Every good thing I have comes from you." I was confused.

Three months after, life in Bong Mines took a turn for the worst. I was too afraid to travel any further, fear of the unknown and what is ahead caused me to have a change of heart. I started making inquiries again on what was the current state of the city because there was news of Peacekeepers from the Economic Community of West African States (ECOWAS) called Economic Community of West African States Monitoring Group (ECOMOG) that was in control of some parts of the city. We were assured that those who would like to return to their homes in the city will be allowed under the protection of ECOMOG.

I, therefore decided to take the risk to return home because I felt there was nothing to stay in Bong Mines for as the condition of life was deteriorating very fast. We took a four days journey from Bong Mines to White Plains. On our way, we slept in abandoned houses, open fields without water and food. I would make trips to catch tiny fish, crabs, and crawfish at times from the nearby stream, creek or river. whatever we caught was the meal for that day. we ate everything that looked edible: sugar cane, cassava roots if available. Being pregnant at such a time was challenging; my entire body felt like giving out especially my legs could no longer provide the support I needed. I was into the third trimester of my pregnancy, we had to use alternate routes to hide from the rebels, there were stories of the rebels raping women and little girls, cutting open the bellies of pregnant women, and performing forms of cannibalism. Those stories and fearful thoughts were overtaking my mind, and I had all the reasons to take all precautionary measures in staying safe when traveling, and the best was again being to travel on foot and very quietly, kids cannot cry, we had to operate in complete silence, and communicated with our heads, eyes, hands, and total body language.

We Finally made it to the border point that separated the peacekeepers from the rebels and we had to walk with our hands in the air to go from the

Rebel side to the other side where the peacekeepers were waiting to receive those who were returning. When we crossed over, I shouted to my kids "we made it! We made it! With tears running down my face. My body was not only rained but I was emotionally and psychologically drained. I was shaking, my voice trembled as I spoke, and I was so weak, to move my legs to another step forward. but the book of Psalm 82:3-4 speaks of God justice "Give justice to the weak and the fatherless; maintain the right of the afflicted and the destitute. Rescue the weak and the needy; deliver them from the hand of the wicked." And this was what God had done for us.

After crossing over, we were taken to our home, but the curfew was still enforced in the City from 7 AM to 7 PM no one came out or could be in the streets between those times. The next day, we worked to make our home livable again; we cleaned and dust around the scraps that were left after the looting. After a complete day of work, I climbed into my bathtub and felt an unusual pain in my abdomen; and realized I was bleeding. my neighbor and I had a signal we used to communicate, her mother was a midwife at the time, I told her what was happening, and she and her mother snuck into my home that night through my back door, her mother cared for me overnight.

The next morning, I was taken to a nearby maternity clinic that was in partial operation; it was operated by a Filipino Doctor, who took me directly into the surgical room. After my initial checkup, he told me I was experiencing a miscarriage. I said, "Oh Lord after all what I went through, I am going to lose my baby." The Doctor did all he could medically to save the baby but prove futile. I was given an emergency Dilation and Curettage commonly known as the D&C procedure. I lost my baby who sex I was told was a boy because of the senseless war that had destroyed our nation.

The situation of losing my baby made me very bitter; I hated the members of all rebel faction groups involved in the war and those attached to them. I wondered how long did I have to hold on in that situation before going into depression again. I thought it was time to dust my feet and leave from the country I have known, a country where love abounded amongst its people, a country where every parent was everyone's parent, a country where we lived as a community of hope. We were loving people, but what went wrong, what had happened, those were questions that still linger in my mind whenever the thought of the war was imagined. It was time to leave. I had no idea where I was headed but I just wanted to leave. As in Philippians 2:13-14, He made a way again, when it seems to be no way, yet in the nick of time God provided a solution, he was my provided, when I needed him to provide, he became my healer when I needed to be healed, he was my sustainer when I needed him to sustain me.

We were able to relocate to a small town at the border of Liberia and the Ivory Coast through the assistance of an eighteen-wheeler truck driver who allowed us through God's favor again to catch a ride in the back of his semi. We stayed in the town for days processing travel documents for the kids and me. I used part of the money given to me by a former classmate SLY. I also made transportation arrangements to continue our journey to the Ivory Coast, where there was no sight of war.

We stayed in the Ivory Coast for about 5 months trying to contact family members in the USA. While in the Ivory Coast, my gift made way for me; I will do hair to sustain the family, this was one thing I did not forget and still knew how to do very well, as mentioned in *Proverbs 18:16- A man's gift makes room for him, and bringeth him before great men.* I was able to gather few clients initially that grew into client retention that I came every three months for a redo.

After several months of no access to communication, we were finally able to get in contact with my mother who informed me that she was told I was killed by a strayed bullet and that all my kids were scattered around the country. We had our moment of tears of joy and catching up. My mother with the assistance of my siblings started the relocation process for us.

We relocated to the refugee camp, Buduburum in Ghana. I would travel from Ghana to the Ivory Coast every three months to meet up my clients for a redo of their hair, which brought me some income. For two years we stayed in the camp we stayed in the camp while our resettlement to the United States was in process.

The kids were enrolled in school and I gradually did hair and became well known as a beautician. I attended a few cosmetology workshops whenever I could afford, and things began to work out fine as we awaited resettlement or immigration process for the U.S. to come to fruition.

Our name finally came up; we completed our interview and our medical examination. A date was given to us for departure and we finally relocated from Ghana to the USA to join the rest of the family.

At this point, I am now a victim of divorce, a young woman who has been physically and mentally abused. I was then age 36. After I relocated to the USA, I was finally able to walk away for good. I did not have to deal with my past life of fear, uncertainty, physical and mental abuse, and torture any longer. I am now in a country that protects against those acts.

LIFE IN THE U.S.

In Wonderland

After a brief struggle with the resettlement process, things took a turn for the best and we were relocated to Atlanta, GA., where I spent about 5-6 years living there with my kids. The thoughts of my struggles of not having enough for my kids and me during the civil crisis back in Liberia, West Africa was blinded by all the goodies the US had to offer, I was fresh out of the way, young, and ready to give life another try, it felt like it was a second chance at life and I wanted to make the best of it for me and my kids. I felt we had gone through the worst and now we could put that behind us.

Little did I know that the US had its own culture shock and challenges, peer pressure on one end and my kids on the other end. The tendency to work as hard as one can to replenish all that was lost during the war, go back to school, and party every weekend were all forces I had to reckon with. I quickly realized doing either of the three takes great sacrifices and time, which would have their share of consequences. One must be very mindful of the choices to be made in these cases when all is handed to you; you will have to choose and choose wisely.

One must set goals and stay focused to reach them. The sooner the better, but better late than never. I choose to go back to school while my kids were in school and work limited hours to enable me spend quality time with them. There were times due to the limited work hours, bills were not paid on time, as a result, the lights were turned off and it did not matter whether it was winter or summer.

You will have to choose which bill was the most important to be paid at a time. I always choose to pay my rent because keeping a roof over the heads of my family was of grave need even in the face of not much to eat.

Speaking of not much to eat, the struggle continues, this it was a new kind of struggle; the struggle of not having enough food or money, the struggle of not meeting the expectation of others. These struggles led me to visit one food banks, one after another, reaching out to different organizations for assistance with the payment of my bills.

I visited the payday loan regularly, and at times would have to take loans from friends and family members, but what God promised back in the war, to supply my needs was also applicable in the great country America. *"Philippians 4:19- and my God will supply every need according to his riches in glory In Christ Jesus"*

My supply came from an unknown source. I was introduced to a beautiful friend and neighbor at the time, Ms. Nelson who took me to a Church that operated a food bank about an hour and a half away from where we lived. The facility became a haven for me and my kids. We went to the church once a week and had to stand in a long line that almost circled the building to get food. It could be snowing, raining, or crushing hot, you could not afford to lose your space in the line.

This went on for about two years as I was still in school, off and on and working limited hours. The food bank alleviated some of my worries of not having enough food to feed my Kids. Therefore, whatever money came in from work paid part of the bills. it was a new kind of struggle. I stayed in school and pushed the wheel till completion. Upon completion of my classes from the Gwinnett County Community college, I got a new job that paid me a bit more than what I was previously making. I was provided a full-time position with a Laboratory Company, and life became a bit stable.

Love Again

Love was in the air again. I was vulnerable, fragile, emotionally drained, afraid of all that had happened, yet I was in a place of desperation and needed someone to provide some form of security. I did not go to the Father, GOD who promised that "I can do all things through Christ who strengthens me – Philippians 4:19" but instead I was going to trust anyone who could provide those needs.

I got into the dating game and that did not go too well for me either, because of my susceptibility I fell for the wrong guy. Don't get me wrong he was a good man, an excellent provider but was the wrong guy for me. Past incidents that involved family members occurred between this guy and some members of my family while I was still in Africa of which I had no clue. It happened that a couple of years back before my coming to the USA, he had dated a family member of mine and part ways years earlier. I had just come to the US and I was mingling and making new friends. After a few months of being around, the situation presented itself and I fell for it innocently. This situation brought about a split in my family, another form of trauma to my life.

I was insulted, talked about in ways one could not imagine. I was shredded to pieces, laughed, and scorned at. I was stuck in that situation for three years because of fear of leaving and not having a home to return to or be welcome into.

Some of what was yearning for in my life was provided to me by outsiders – friends and acquaintance; they showed me love by visitation, calls, and even hung out with me. However, nothing could take away the emptiness I felt for not receiving love from the people I trusted. The pain of isolation from my loved ones was taking me through a lot. I only had my mother and oldest brother to rely on; they were the only ones I could call and felt comfortable speaking with. When the people you expect to show you love and forgiveness turn their backs on you and you have nowhere to turn, remember Psalm 27:10 "when my mother and father forsake me, the Lord will take me in" It is a promise in the scripture that you can be forsaken by your nearest and dearest, you will not be forsaken by the Lord.

The situation became so overwhelming that I turned to alcohol for relief, which only gave me a temporary feel good but didn't take away the reality of life that I had to face daily. Slowly, I was slipping into depression and I started to stay home all the time. I did not want people to see me in public for I felt judged one way or the other whenever they saw me. The devil reminded me of how worthless I was, how nothing good could come out of me, how dirty I was, and how much of a no-good person I was, but there was a reassurance when *"Jesus said unto her, who are those accusers, let them throw the first stone- John 8:10,"* For me, my accusers did not cease; they continued tirelessly to drag me in the mud. Have you ever been disappointed in the people you expect to show you so much love, especially the ones close to your heart? This was where I found myself at that time, but thanks be to God that he makes a way every time and all the time. He is the present help when we are in need.

As I was clinging on for security and love, I was cheated on. The news spread quickly in the community and the humiliation from my accusers and those I loved went wild. Folks I considered friends at the time destroyed me, even those that did not know me had a lot to say about me in private and in public gatherings. It did not matter if I was present or not, they had the satisfaction of dragging my name in the mud, deforming my character in my presence and that of my children at times, my religious beliefs were even questioned. At this lowest time in my life, it felt like I had committed the worst crime ever and did not deserve to be a part of society. I had to make a firm and sound decision to have a turning point in my life. When you feel that all is lost, and you have nowhere to run or hide, remember who God says you are, what are his thoughts and promises for you for He is a God of the second chance.

Soul Searching

I returned to church, visited the mid-week and Sunday services. I started my soul-searching journey. I was a lost daughter who was trying to find her way back to the only man she knew, Jesus who has not disappointed, failed, disgraced, or cast her away. During the process, I was reminded that God was not my accuser and He still loved me, and his precious arms were stretched open for my return. The devil was my accuser, as he is always.

For me to regain my place as a daughter who Christ had given his life on the cross for and be reunited with my Father, the everlasting Father, I needed to come clean by acknowledging what I had innocently partaken of, that has resulted into the names calling, and character deformation. Overall, I needed to make no excuses but to come before God and confessing my sins, asking for forgiveness and forgiving those that had caused me so much hurt.

God began my restoration process by allowing me to separate myself from the place the situation had occurred. I was to stay away from the people I loved but had caused me so much hurt and pain. The urge to do so was heavier each day I attempted to stay and not obeying what God was instructing me to do.

My Path To Restoration

I relocated to Dallas, TX. My oldest daughter was expecting her first child at the time and she also lived in TX. I figured it could be the best option to start over, my search and quest for a resolution to all that I had gone through in life: the disappointment, degradation, humiliation, fear, instability, negativity, and trauma. I was overcome by stress; henceforth, I wanted to go somewhere I could hide, where no one knew me, somewhere new, where I could start my life over and redo my life path if I could.

The Prodigal Daughter

Like the story told in the Bible in Luke chapter 15 about the prodigal son, I knew that which I was seeking out there, my Father, God had them in abundance. All I needed was to return home. While going through these situations of life, I drifted from the first love I have always known. I knew my Father; God's arms were wide open to receive me whenever I returned. I do believe when I return to my Father he will rejoice because it is written in the scriptures when *"one sinner repents, heaven rejoices."* I believed that the day; I returned heaven rejoiced and there was a great celebration as inscribed in scripture.

Coming home to my father was not the end; it was the initial step my process to my restoration. I had to search for a church, one I will call my home, family oriented, a church that would not compromise the word of God; I needed to hear straight talk, the truth from the scriptures, a church that would provide guidance to my new walk, and a better relationship with my Lord and Savior Jesus Christ.

I was in search of a church that would not hear my story and question or judge me, a church family that would not see my past but see the beauty of God's creation in and through me, and that was when found the New Life Fellowship Church, located in Euless TX, where Bishop Nathan S. Kortu presides over the duties and functions of the saints.

By the grace of God, through the principles instilled in me by my late father, Mr. Christopher T. S. Cole, and the mentorship of Bishop Nathan S. Kortu, a man endowed with the anointing and wisdom of God, I was cultivated and shaped into the God-fearing women I am today. Bishop Nathan S. Kortu did not only mentor me spiritually as a spiritual head, he also provided a father-daughter relationship I lost when the cold hands of death took away my beloved Papa after a brief illness on December 2, 2000.

The spiritual values instilled in me by my biological father, Mr. C. T. S. Cole from an early age enhanced the quest to return to those things that made me feel fulfilled. Those values from my parents began to gradually resurface as my search continued, my spiritual head Bishop Nathan Kortu unfolded the fruitfulness of indulging into the word of God. The intense beauty and importance of staying in the presence of the Lord were realized. The awesomeness of his power to transform and renew what was once considered a mess into a message and a time of test into a life of testimony was emotionally strong. Life began to feel normal, but this type of normality was different, it felt resolve, it felt real, it felt complete, it felt right and renewed. I was willing to go deeper and see what was in it for me if the promises of God applied to me too. I played all these thoughts in my mind over and again trying to believe and not to believe, because of what the enemy had told me, and accuse me of. Revelation 12:10 speaks of the "devil been the accuser of the brethren before God day and night."

A NEW CHAPTER

I served several years on the praise and worship team, in the choir, in the women ministry, and was a two-term voting board member. I attended months of intense training, seminars, serving on the church board, performing my call to duty, and walking in obedience with the scripture under the leadership of the present Presiding Bishop of the New Life Fellowship Church in Euless, TX, Bishop Nathan S. Kortu and members of the leadership board began the process towards my ordination. After months of observation, and examination, I was ordained and licensed as a minister of the gospel in October of 2006. My new role as an ordained minister came with more responsibilities and challenges.

Wolves In Sheep Clothing

All that glitters is not gold (Dryden, 1687). After years of seeking God for a partner, I meet an individual who seemed too ready to settle down. I was introduced to his family and he was introduced mine. We went on dates, traveled to places, made new friends, and as it is often said: "all seemed to be too good to be true." Ladies be on the alert for red flags in all relationships you involved yourself with. If you are a true child of God, what you ask for you shall receive, God will open your eyes to see into the deep secrets of the heart of man, you will just have to depend on him through your prayers.

After a year of dating, we got engaged on, December 2, 2007. He planned the engagement on a Sunday morning having eleven women from my church to give me roses. Each rose represented a beautiful quote that he had provided to them; they were read as the names of the ladies were called and handed to me. The engagement was elaborate, and I was flattered by his kind gestures. We afterward set the date for the wedding. Months after the engagement, I began to suspect some things that came by way of excuses and complaints. However, these signs were due to the initial boundaries I had set in place and was agreed upon by both parties involved, to simply live the rules of abstinence – no sex before marriage, or we go our separate ways, I did not want to keep making mistakes or having regrets of these kinds any longer. Doing the same thing and having the same result over a period required a change in the process.

The request to go clubbing was continuously made, and my response was "I don't go clubbing because it is not what my lifestyle has been." Remember, now I am already ordained and occupying key roles in the church. I should be a role model because much is expected of me from those under my leadership. The book of Luke 12:48 speaks of "For unto whomsoever much is given of him, shall much be required. I was expected to live up to the standards of the scriptures, and I vowed to never go down the road of disobedience anymore.

My mind was becoming confused and uncertainty began to set in. I started questioning myself about my decision if it was the right thing to take this individual to become a life partner. I did what I only knew to do, fast and pray. I asked God for clarity and the day came, my answers were written on the wall in the color red. Be mindful of your relationship with the things concerning the Father, He will act on your behalf if you call unto him in sincerity.

Some issue came up that had to be handled. I took one of the cars to the shop for repairs. I was the driver for that day and had to provide a ride for the individual after work on that day. On my way, I got a call that the individual was on the bus instead, 25 minutes later I got another call from the same phone, but this time it was another voice on the other line. It was the voice of a bus driver, and he asked if I knew who owned the phone? I responded, "yes, and give a brief description of the phone and the individual." I asked the bus driver why he was asking, he stated, "that the individual who owns the phone got off the bus and left the phone on the seat." And that he the driver did not notice the phone on the seat until later, so he decided to call the last dialed number on the phone. I provided additional information, we both decided to meet at the nearest point which was a Blockbuster store nearby. After about 10 minutes the bus driver drove into the parking lot, I introduced myself to him and he gave me the phone. From the moment the phone was handed to me it did not stop ringing, text messages were coming in back to back, including pictures.

I decided to respond to some of the calls and text messages, but that was a huge mistake because of things I was hearing and seeing from the calls and texts were unimaginable. Many things began to circulate my mind and I asked myself "if I am ready to get married in a couple of months?" I asked "why? No answers were coming forth." This was the beginning of the closure of that relationship for me, I realized it was ok to let go at this point, and don't hold on to stuff that was already falling apart, the trust was gone.

I was in tears for days, I asked: "God why me?" As hard as it was, I began to give God the glory and He began to comfort me with different scriptures. One scripture that stock with me was *Deuteronomy 31:6 "Be strong and courageous, do not be afraid, the Lord God goes with you, he will never leave you nor forsake you."* Even thou I believe those words, they only encouraged me temporarily. I was so devastated and decided that this Christian walk was no longer for me. I said, "I did, and is doing everything right before you God, why me." We tend to ask the WHY ME question when things are not going our way, which way are we going to choose, God's way or your way, if we say God knows what's best for us, then why do we always ask the question, we must allow him to lead us on the right path.

It was on a Saturday night I got dressed and decided to go out and do whatever felt right in my eyes out of frustration. Our quick decisions will bring us setbacks in most cases and we will suffer the consequences. But when God has his hands on your life, He will protect you in ways unimaginable for His promises to be fulfilled in your life and purpose. He protected me in an unbelievable manner, he did by allowing my daughters to stop by for a visit and left one of my grandsons to hang out with me while they were gone to the store, they took so long that the baby fell asleep.

I put the baby to bed and was waiting on their return when I began to feel sorry for myself for what I was experiencing. I realized going out to do whatever out of frustration was not the solution. Tears rolling down my cheeks, I fell on my knees before my bed still fully dress and began to cry to God in prayers. I later found myself in that same position on that night because God knew what I was planning to do on that night was not pleasant in his sight, and that there was a place of rest in him, so he protected me.

The next morning, I woke up and realized my daughters had returned and gotten the baby. I did not understand what had happened me. God had taken me into a deep sleep; like it was a mandatory rest.

I went to the shower in preparation if Sunday service and the tears started rolling again. God comforted me and assured me that it was not over; He loved me, and it was going to get better, and that my latter would be better than my former. He blessed me with these words while I was in the shower: "it's going to work out in my favor once again," God gave me additional words that were written into a song. Today that song is the number one song on my first album. What a Father that cares so much for his children, when we feel down and low, disappointed and discourage, he is there, when we feel all is lost, he is there, he protects his own.

At times when we are in a place of disappointment and desperation, we have the tendency to feel alone but God is close enough to hear our payers. He is closer than you think, His ears are always available to hear us, his eye are always, always watching over us, and his arms are always open to receive us. We must be knowledgeable of what is available to us through the word of God in the midst of our desperation and failures. The enemy is very clandestine and crafty in his actions, be mindful of sheep in wolves clothing, resist the devil and he will flee from you.

This was the power of God working on my behalf; He will give you what you ask in sincerity, in the book of James 4:2 God said: *"you receive not because you ask not, seek and ye shall find, knock and it shall be open unto you."*

I asked him for clarity and he gave me all the answers I needed within days. He is still in the protection business, he wants to protect our little hearts always. We just need to be able to allow him to come in and do the mending for us. *In Psalm 105:15 "he said touch, not my anointed ones and do my prophets no harm."*

Questioning My Faith

Sometimes doing the right thing hurts worst, and you tend to question your faith. You are doing everything right, yet your faith takes a hit and you are discouraged, disappointed, apprehensive, frustrated and fear sets in…. but don't write me off just yet, because I am in the same place as others are. I am in the same carriage, a human like everyone else. I go through tough times also. When it gets tough and your faith takes a strike. What do you do? Do you run and hide, or trust God and keep standing after you have done all you can in your little power.

The enemy speaks in your ears and reminds you of all the commitment you have made to God, yet things are not working for you. You are getting absolutely no result What do you say or do at that moment? You must remind the devil of your choice to keep walking the walk and talking the talk. You continue to dwell under the shadow of the Almighty. It is not an easy task to live the life as a born-again believer, to have a personal relationship with God, to live a life of integrity can cost a lot. Saints, don't allow the devil to shut you up, speak the truth and live the truth *"for it is only the truth that will set you free –John 8:32."*

The Blessing of A Great Partner

Don't be discouraged if folks don't see the God in you; they don't respect you, and they speak ills of you. Just be the child of God that you were made to be. Don' try to be someone else; be who God made you be. David sat in the fields by himself; he was only known as the shepherd boy. He had seven brothers in the same home with his father, yet none of his brothers recognized who he was. It took a prophet to show up to announce who David was. You can be in the same house/home, the same church, organization, or in your family, yet those around you don't recognize what you carry or who you are in the sight of God. I want to assure you that God sees you and all your potentials, there is a prophet on his way to point you out, stay faithful to what you believe, for its Christ who is our solid rock, all others are sinking sand, God will gradually unfold who you are by what he will do through you, that those around you will see and will join to celebrate you.

After three years of no dating but a commitment to just the things of God, He blessed me with a wonderful partner, it was an express package. We had long talks for some time and had stated our expectations, I told him where I stood with my relationship with God and will not compromise it for no one and he was included. There is a saying in Africa that "If you have been burned before, you will take all necessary precautions to prevent another fire from igniting". It was one night he drove from Atlanta where he lived at the time for 14 hours unknowingly to me. I got a call about 3 AM on a February morning, it was his voice on the other line. He asked me for my address that he wanted to mail something to my home; I provided my address and wondered why he was still up so late, but eventually went back to sleep, after about an hour I got a knock on my door. I answered the door with the question "who you are knocking my door at this time" and he responded, "your husband." I went through the whole nine to make sure he was who he said he was, and that was the beginning of a beautiful story and a wonderful relationship, that was the beginning of my fairy tale, that I am living presently. You don't have to be wealthy to live a fairy tale life, it will depend on your definition of what that is.

Two days of his arrival, he took me on a ride downtown not knowing we were going to get our marriage license, another surprise. Look when God is in it, there is no stress, no doubt, and no complaint. He will do what he has promised, "*he is not a man to lie.*" Numbers 23:19. It is so true that "*my latter is by far better than my former.*"

After counseling we got married and decided to relocate to the East Coast Queens, New York precisely after a year. It was a very challenging time for me as I have never been away from my kids, and I am now faced with the decision to either accompany my husband in his endeavors which will enhance our financial status or stay with my kids to be the mother and grandmother that I already was. At this time three of the kids are already college students and one was about to graduate from high school in a couple of months.

I was also left with another important decision, which was leaving my church where I have served and played very important roles in parts of the ministry for many, many years. My husband and I meet with the Senior Pastor at the time, Pastor Nathan S. Kortu and discussed our plans for relocating to New York. He told us he was going to allow God to have his will in the situation. After praying for some time concerning the situation, Pastor Nathan S Kortu at the time gave me the release from participating in activities of the church to accompany my husband.

According to Ephesians 5:21-24 and 1Corinthians 11:3 "the word speaks of the husband being the head of the home as Christ is the head of the church." I was married now, the fact that my husband was seeking to improve our lives, granted that he needed all my support, we spoke with the kids about our plans. It did not go too well for they were not used to the separation part, but we came to a common understanding. They all had their own homes and lives, except for the one who was about to get out of high school, my prayer was for God to take over my children, that he will complete that which he has started, regardless of where I was he will take care of my children. My assurance is in Christ.

The day finally came, and we are all set out to leave on an almost a two days journey, then it hit me hard that I was leaving the only people I knew for all my life. I was leaving people who have stood by and with me, people that have gone through with me, the people who have defended me, who have fought for and with me, people who loved me unconditionally. I was already missing them while l was still in Texas.

As tears were flowing, my phone rang, it was my spiritual father, Pastor Nathan on the other line. He began to pray for me, giving me his blessings and finally told me that it was God's will for me to leave to support my husband. He told me that God had already placed people in my path that will make an impact in my life, some will come to stay, and some will come and leave, but my decision to relocate was divinely orchestrated by God. I did not understand it then but as time went by it all began to unfold revelation one after another.

We made the two days trip and finally got to New York, and things were falling into place as expected, my husband started classes. In the midst of all that was happening, I had some challenges with my in-laws, that quickly subsided after his classes were over and we move to the New Jersey area. Then came a new set of challenges, no Job and many bills to be paid. There were times my husband had interviews and he was told he was the best fit for the position and was later told he did not get the Job. Your marriage will be tested in every form, shape, and color.

There was one instance I remember very well, it was with a Jewish company in New York city with excellent pay and benefits. My husband was to start on the following Monday and got a call on Friday before that he did not get the job. I immediately ran into my room and began to question God, I began to remind him of his promises, and what He said a husband should be to his family, and that he cannot do those things without him being financially equipped. I reminded God of his promises in Philippians 4:19 that he *"will supply all my needs according to his riches in glory in Christ Jesus."*

Seeking God In Your Place of Desperation

I went into seven days of fasting and praying, believing God for a change. I continued to remind Him of all his promises. God had assured me that it will be well in due time, we must apply the scriptures to our lives daily and remind God of his promises towards us. I shook the enemy's kingdom in blasting prayers and pronouncements and got the victory over my situation. I got a call on the seventh day from a friend who was serving in the position of a manager at a company in Philadelphia, the company serves individuals with developmental disabilities. We talked for a while and I told her I was job hunting. She told me what she did as the manager and what was required of those who worked with her, she then provided me with some information about the application and hiring process.

I shared the information with a friend and loved ones with the detail of the job was, and I was again put down by these words and I quote "*You are going to join the van wagon of those cleaning folks in the nursing home. Why do you want to work for pennies instead of dollars?*" The enemy will always find ways to bring discouragement into our situation, but we must know the word of God and know it for ourselves, that we can answer back and bring his intentions to full stop.

I told myself this is not the end but just the beginning of my purpose. I will use my opposition as my elevation, people will put you down and discourage you from achieving your purpose in life, but like the women with the issue of blood in the book of Matthew 9:20-22, Mark 5:25-34, and Luke 8:43-48, stand strong. I stood my grounds and reminded myself of all the promises that God had for my life, and stepped out in faith, and he has never failed me yet, use your haters as your elevators.

I went ahead and applied for the job, after a week I was called for an interview, went for the interview and was hired on the spot. Folks in the book of Numbers 23:19 *says "that God is not a man that he should lie, neither a son of man that he should repent, what he said, and shall he not do it, or hath he spoken, and shall he not make it good."* What God says he will do, his promises will surely come to pass. Oh, what a mighty God we serve!

What is the height of your desperation, when you are in the place of despair, it becomes a now-thing, a now breakthrough, and a now healing. When you need a now result, you cannot afford to be correct politically, you don't need to be validated by no human, can't be proper, and you cannot be concerned with what folks will say about you; they will judge you anyways. You just need a now-miracle, so go and get it. HALLELUJAH!! I feel like having church!

I left home for work on Mondays and returned on Fridays. My husband was still not working, after two months on the job, the company was about to conduct another job fair. I told my husband about the job fair, he reluctantly attended cause my husband is a guy who likes to get his hands dirty; he is a handyman, being an HVAC, EPA certified professional, he did not see himself working at a desk on a computer with a printer around him but when God gets ready you will move as He wishes for you.

My husband attended the job fair and was offered a managerial position. I said to my husband, I have been with this company for over two months and you just came and you are offered a managerial position. "If God be for you who can be against you." He started in his new role as a manager and eventually loved every bit of it.

We moved into a suburb of Philadelphia, where we could be close to work.

My desire to praise and worship God began to increase. I found myself praising and worshiping as thoughts of the goodness of God ran through my mind. I would sit and write songs for my library only, never dreamt of recording an album, I wrote only for my enjoyment.

I did a short YouTube video as a habit. My former choir director called me and while chatting, he asked: "have you ever thought of recording the song you have written?" I said, "No, I don't have that in mind at all." He then talked me into reaching out to another guy in Staten Island New York and this guy referred me to another guy who was a producer in the Philadelphia. God was unfolding another reason for my relocation to the East Coast, and I was paying keen attention.

I spoke with the producer, Mr. Prince Thomas Sherman, AKA Just prince. We immediately connected and set a date to meet. The chemistry between us was so divinely apparent, we both busted into a time of worship in the studio, and I gave birth to my first song on the album "It's going to work in my favor". To date, I have recorded two albums of which Mr. Prince T. Sherman produced. My producer is a blessing to my music ministry, it all came together because of his obedience to God to be a blessing to me, when God set the stage for you, the rest will be history, allow him to steer your boat or sale you ship, and the winds and waves will have nothing on you because the Master is in charge.

I want to admonish you that no one stands in the way of what God has set to do in your life. When God gets ready, He will move the earth and set it in place just because of you, that's the God that I serve. He moves mountains, walks on water, he heals the sick, and raises the dead, he is God all by himself.

My Mother Last Days

I move to Philadelphia during the early stage of my mother's illness, at the time she resided on the east coast. We would go to visit, spend weekends at times, her Illness grew worst and it came to a point that she needed additional help with her daily activities. I had just taken a vacation leave from work at the time, so I volunteered to drive back and forth to give her the needed assistance.

My vacation was coming to an end, but I saw the greater need to continue providing the needed assistance to my mother. My siblings and I discussed the situation and I agreed to take up the task to travel three hours daily, an hour and a half one way for three days a week. I did that for a couple of months and later reduced commute time to two days a week. I would do three days off and on as needed.

After months of visitation, doctor's appointments, picking up medication, doing laundry, having some very important conversation, and learning new things from my mommy, the reality was sinking in that her health was gradually depreciating, I stayed close and pay more attention to get as much wisdom from her cause the reality was she would not be around longer. Her illness took a turn for the worst, she would complain at times, she cried about the way she felt and looked. I would offer words of encouragement, played music and sometimes sing an old song she knew, and talked about old stories that made her feel a bit better. On one visit I remember her asking me to get a bag from the basement and take it to her room, she knew I loved to sew, she told me to open the bag I did and found pieces of materials nicely folded and well packed, I came across a baby blue lace, she stopped me and said "if anything happens to me and I don't make it through this illness, make sure what ever you all decide, make sure to give me my wishes to laid me to rest in a baby blue gown, blue just like the color I was holding." I asked, "why are you speaking in such a manner?" She just smiled and said "I am serious," I said "ok." She had an emergency that took her to the hospital and she was admitted for some time.

My grandkids came up to spend some time with me in 2014. We took off on Thanksgiving Day to visit my mom at the hospital, she had been admitted a day before. We got to the hospital and she was excited to see the kids, we hung out with her for hours. She shared her food with the kids and was giving them some pieces of advice. She looked better, very relaxed but still did not look very well, little did I know that would be the last time I would see her alive. She was discharged on the Friday after Thanksgiving and gained her wings on Saturday night on December 6th, 2014.

It was a painful moment, but also thankful that another reason for my relocation was acknowledged. I was to be on the East coast to assist in taking care of my mother during her illness. I could not have had that opportunity of blessing had I still been in Texas, I would have been restricted on how long I could stay. It was an opportunity of a lifetime to be able to take care of an aging parent who was ill.

It was all joyful spending her last days with her, I saw her pain, listened to her complaints, listen to her frail voice when she was not feeling her best, I gave her showers, seeing her smile when she was in a good place, listened to her pray for her children, friends, and herself every day. When she was unable she would call the prayer line and just hold the phone to her ears. Everyone in the family knew not to call her between 9 PM and 10 PM, she will be praying at that time. I miss her dearly, but she is in a better place now, where she will experience no pain or discomfort, oh my mommy was a darling a princess with a beautiful soul. I missed my mama, yet I know her memories will continue to live on in our hearts. It was my pride and joy to have experienced the time with her, and I can write a book about our time together. I am blessed to have had this opportunity.

The Challenge of Returning To School

I made a firm and wise decision to return to school. However, returning to school to do my MBA turned out to be exciting, bumpy, time-consuming, and entertaining. Moreover, I struggled with the formidable of my insecurities as to whether I would be able to stand the test of time since I was returning to school after so many years. I feared not having the time, energy, not catching on in time or been able to comprehend the materials.

I was afraid and began to overthink the fact of been in school again. It was frightening. Often we see the different stages and episodes of life, like age, caring for our kids, or getting involved with our jobs becomes a stumbling block to enhancing our education or whatever career we find ourselves consumed with, but those I consider fears or distractions.

Philippians 4:13 states "*I can do all things through Christ which strengthens me.*" I am reminded of this scripture that I can do all things through Christ who gives me strength, now why should I allow my progress to be delayed or be distracted by fear, he has not given the spirit of fear but of love and of sound mind. Going back to school was one of the things included in all the things I could do through Christ, I thought to take the bold step of going back to school.

Even though I played Philippians. 4:13 in my head over and again, somewhere in the back of my mind, I still had that fear lingering. I was filled with unpredictability whether this initiative to return to school will afford me a better position in the workforce or afford me some financial stability to my family after graduation that would make staying in it for the long haul worth the experience and effort.

There were times I will hire a tutor to assist me with my school work; I would make calls to my professor and request extensions on the time to return assignments, and at times I sought assistance from my kids. My assurance and support came from my husband, my bishop, and my children, those two years was not an easy journey but was made possible through the grace of God and the people he placed in my life.

Returning to school opened doors to my careers that would not have been possible otherwise. I quickly realized the importance of not getting embroiled in my present situation, but rather enhance my educational status. Enhancing your status educationally puts you in a completely different class and gives you a ton of options. Note, an educated woman who feared the Lord is an incredible force to reckon with because she has the power to influence destinies and to lead people to righteous living.

I am appreciative that I took the chance; I am grateful I persevered through the bad and good times. There were days when I could not cope with the pressure of thinking of my mother's illness, or answering my teammates on a project, turning in my assignment on time, or work and school. During that time and overall, I was overwhelmed with just the whole process, but I made it and eventually completed my MBA. Yeah, I did! Paul said in Philippians 3:12 "*about pressing on to take hold of that for which Christ took hold of me.*"

At this point in my life, I can legitimately say it was well worth the ride. As you scan for new possibilities, you will experience unbelievable emotional struggles, you must stand firm and fight head on, if not fulfilling your dreams will never be possible. As you overcome one challenge at a time, God is equipping you for the greater task ahead.

After obtaining my MBA, I was now ready to conquer the world. I sought the Father, God for His will and vision for my future. He told me to move in a new direction, I made up my mind to go all the way with Him and didn't mind where he was taking me. Today I am enjoying the discovery of sailing into a new season, and it feels awesome.

The Closure I Craved

The pain of losing a child is unimaginable, I wish this for no one, not even my enemies. I had thoughts of what would have been the future of the child, my memory will go in and out, the pain started to emerge, I did not want to remember the pain I was constantly feeling, for years I carried that pain and did not speak of it or told anyone of what I was experiencing, I will have dreams, dreams that will wake me up at night and I will be in tears, this continued for many years.

Until the year 2014 when I decided to take a trip home to get some closure to all that has happened in my life during the war, I was afraid, afraid of the unknown, fear of having the feelings I had before, fear of everything, but I wanted this trauma to come to an end, the book of *2Timothy 1:7 states "God hath not given us the spirit of fear, but of power and of love and of sound mind.*

I Finally made the trip to the mother land with the encouragement of my husband, I did what I needed to do, visited the places I needed to visit, and spoke with those I had to speak with, and I receive the closure I always desired, but there was a need that was realized in the process that was nowhere near my agenda, God opened my eyes and allowed me to see the need to help young women/ youth in my country, we have our plans but God has a purpose for each and every one of his children, *Isaiah 55:8 "For my thoughts are not your thoughts, neither your ways mine"*, I had found mine and birth a non-profit called the Women /Youth Development and Empowerment Fund (WYDEF), This is an endeavor I always wanted to take on but did not know where to start or how. God had given me the opportunity and it was time to move in that direction.

Making Generational Impact

I am presently preaching, speaking, singing, teaching the word of God, and assisting less fortunate individuals in third world countries through my non- profit organization, the Women and Youth Development and Empowerment Fund (WYDEF), established in 2014, is a 501c3 status organization based both in the United States and Liberia. Being able to make a difference in one's life every day is an accomplishment. I believe serving others is what I am called to do.

The fear of failure will incapacitate your mind and disable your very thoughts if you think your performances should compare to other individual who are successful, because of thoughts of not meeting your goals, or what if things don't go as expected.

What if the organization never gets from ground level? We know what our community or society expects of us, but we never ask ourselves what is God's expectation for us.

In Titus 3:8, *"good works are excellent and profitable to everyone."* God's purpose for his children is to obtain the maximum use of our talents and gifts. As Colossians 3:23 puts it *"Whatever you do work heartily as for the Lord and not for men."* God has immensely blessed me with many gifts and applying these gifts has been a challenge for the fear of having negative thoughts, and many what "if's" began to surface but I refused to be held back by negative thoughts and I believe that I can achieve whatever I put my mind to in accordance to God's purpose and plans. I did not and do not allow impractical assumptions to cripple my thoughts or hindered my actions.

Regardless of where you are in life, use the gifts that God has entrusted to you, be it in your home, work environment, church, or in your community. Trusting and obeying God with the Holy Spirit in all you do will cause you to attain distinction.

I began to pray for the opportunity to serve. I wanted to challenge myself to get out of the box, leave the familiar and walk into the unfamiliar, which was to serve other women.

I wanted to serve women who are experiencing what I have experienced and help them become overcomers. I knew they needed to hear from someone who has been there, someone who understood what it meant to lose all that she has ever worked for, who has gone through losing a family member: child, mother, father, best friend, a woman that has gone without food for days, who knew how to feed her kids with the little she had and went to bed hungry for days, and knows what it meant to walk for days and have split heels, a woman who had withstood the test of time; I was so ready to tell my story and bless someone.

I wanted to give something back, some form of relief to the less fortunate women in my community and country. I was fortunate to have come to the great United States of America. I was able to rebuild over the years and now ready for the opportunity to return the favor God has bestowed upon me to other women.

The desire to give back to my community was immense. I took off with the non-profit organization here in the USA after it was previously registered in Liberia, West Africa. The real work started, sitting back was not in my book, I needed to do this, nothing was going to stop me. I was tested many times to keep going or to quit, but quitting was not an option. I was in this all the way and I prevailed with God's guidance and the support of my loving husband and few others.

I completed the registration, the By-Laws, and constitution, completed the incorporation process, and later obtained the tax-exempt status 5O1(C3) all within a year plus. This was with the assistance and ingenuity of my spiritual father the Presiding Bishop of the New Life Fellowship Church, Bishop Nathan S. Kortu, who is also the present board chairman of the organization, WYDEF.

To date, I am assisting young ladies through high school, college, and undertaking annual projects, fundraiser dinners, female hygiene products drive, and back to school drive. Our sympathizers or donors are given the opportunity to make donations and contributions to the cause. We also undertake the "Feed the Children Project" (FTC), this project feeds about 300 children in Africa over the Christmas holidays.

I am excited to see those things that have always been a dream now becoming a reality; "with God all things are possible,". It's okay to be uncomfortable before being comfortable, its ok to go through the storms of life and come out victorious

My passion gives me the inspiration to get the job done. My motivation pushes me to do the things I thought was impossible, it gives me the drive to produce better results through serving. When I feel the fear of not reaching my goal to serve, I am sustained and reminded of what drives me and I tell myself tomorrow will be a better day. I never lost my love for humanity which has always been my guiding principle and primary duty.

I have never been the one that was good at sales, but my inspiration to serve others especially the less fortunate, the love of God, and the joy that comes with serving has given me the stimulation to fulfill my services.

To serve is to render assistance, to be of help, to answer the purpose, to be useful, to render obedience, to answer the call, to provide, to do a duty. I am also a believer that it is my duty as a part of the Army of Christ to serve; I am glad the opportunity presented itself and I ran with it. Initially, I was a bit skeptical about making the attempt and taking the risk, if service is not given as a calling from God, you will burn out very easily because you are serving in the flesh.

The bible verses below speak about God's expectations for us as believers when we are in the called business of serving.

I Samuel 12:24, but be sure to fear and serve the LORD faithfully and with all

your heart. Galatians 5:13, Serve one
another humbly and in Love; Hebrews
6:10, God is not unjust; he will not
forget your work and the love you have
shown him as you have served his people
and continue to help them.

When one is thinking of becoming a server, it is wise to seek the guidance of God before branching into that area. It takes great sacrifice and endurance to serve. When serving one will encounter temptation from those you are servicing, and those that work with you.

As I serve, I am learning to exercise more patience with those I work with and serve. I have come to realize that patience is of great importance, first and foremost in serving. During serving one will encounter negative situations such as dishonesty, immoral conducts, unappreciative behaviors, and more. The server must be equipped for the task ahead. The way one resolves those temptations will be influenced by one's relationship with God.

Some of the greatest joy and moments of my life is not when I receive but it's when I give. We must serve a purpose. Remember, Jesus Christ before the final moment of His life, he decided to serve and wash the feet of his disciples. We must find where we fit in God's purpose.

What is serving and how does one serve? One cannot serve with their own agenda until they are willing to put away their agenda and take on God's agenda. We cannot serve with the tenacity and urgency required without being in the will of God. We must be in the will and purpose of God to serve.

Selfish people don't serve; they don't serve the Lord, their family, their community, their neighbors, or their generation. Selfish people want to be served and get served. They will even critique the way they are served, and they have high standards on what it requires to please them. They never consider they are to be serving, but if the God that we worship serves, then there is no position or level of standard that should exempt us from serving.

When we place ourselves on the receiving end, we realize collecting stuff brings us little or no joy. When we just collect and not give in return, we miss out on experiencing the position to serve or give. What a rewarding feeling, Jesus Christ himself went down on his knees and wash the feet of his disciples –John 13:1-17.

Life demands us to be servants, we must train our children to be servants. You serve first and you will be served in a long run. Money follows serving. When you serve there are possibilities you will always have a job because people remember the services you rendered. Are you a servant, what will people miss you when you are no more? What will they miss you for when you are no more?

Duet 8:11, God is reminding us about how he serves us in the wilderness and against all odds. He still makes provisions. If we can only remember where he has brought us, we must have a servant's heart, giving must be a way of life. It is a blessing to be in the position to be of service to others. Serving is an honor unto God.

Life Shocking Moment

When life seems to be going well, and you feel you have all your ducks in order, there is no time for distraction. Suddenly, you get a strike with the least on your list, like an unknown illness and everything changes. One minute all is well at home and the next you are hospitalized, and you began to ask yourself "how did I get here?" We must be vigilant and in readiness to meet our Savior always. The famous quote "Tomorrow is not promised to anyone" resonates, but while it is true that tomorrow is not promised to anyone the scripture tells us in Psalm 90:10, "*the days of our years are threescore years and ten; and if by reason of strength they be fourscore years.*"

With the numbers in the scriptures, we can be assured that the promise is ours as children of God. We must do all that is necessary to assure the fulfillment of this promise, eating right, resting, exercising, doctor visits the whole time. I am saying all these above and the question of "how I got here?" still lingers in my mind.

It was on a hot summer Thursday around 4:00 PM when I got some food to eat. After a couple of spoons fills, I felt a strange pain in my abdomen, not too alarming. I continued to go about my normal duties, but as the hours went by the pain increased and deepen into that night; it became unbearable. I woke up and reached for some pain pill, took the pain pills and after about an hour the pain subsided.

I was finally able to get some sleep. Friday came it was a beautiful day, I went to do my morning walk as I always did and noticed something strange. I could not complete the trail I have been walking for over a month. I was exhausted and feeling very tired. I wondered why and just alluded it to the rough night I had. Are we paying attention to our bodies? If yes, what is it saying to us? If no, then why are we not listening?

I am presently growing through various changes in my body as I am growing older. Whether mental, emotional, physical, or spiritual changes, nature has a way of handing these changes down to us and we must decide what to do with them.

My body was speaking to me on that Thursday, but I didn't pay much attention. The pain became severe, then came the high fever of 104, nausea, and diarrhea. Due to the intensity of my symptoms, my husband rushed me to the emergency department of the Jefferson Memorial Hospital located downtown Philadelphia. The condition led to my hospitalization for four days. Four days of various testing, MRI, antibiotics, and an administered blood transfusion due to the dropping of my hemoglobin the number was as low as 6.9.

I was dying slowly, but during my fear of the unknown, I was reminded of God's promises, in the book of Psalm 90:10 "speaks of his promises of threescore and ten and if by strength fourscore." God restored my health.

My Present Life

I obtained my MBA in June of 2015, I am currently a candidate for the Doctor of Theology program at the CICA International University and Seminary in New York. I am married to a wonderful man Mr. Samuel H Hardy, God has blessed us with our children and grandchildren. I have no complaints, he supports me in all I do, including ministry work, checking on our children/grandchildren, school work and other things that are of importance to our family. I look forward to the lead of God and all that He wants me to accomplish in my time here on Earth. The legacy you create today will be remembered when you are no more, try to leave one as it is important to those you represent, and represent you. GOD BLESS ALL.

Printed in the United States
By Bookmasters